$\mathcal{W}$EDDING STATIONERY

*W*EDDING STATIONERY

The Easy Instructional DVD Book

This *Show Me How* DVD Book explains how to plan,
style and make your own beautiful stationery for a
wedding and a wedding reception.

The book is designed to be used together with the DVD,
which includes filmed demonstrations of each of the
featured invitation cards, plus the basic skills you need.

Each project and basic skill on the following pages
is cross-referenced to the DVD menu, making it easy
to go straight to the demonstration you need.

SHOW
ME
HOW

Show Me How – Wedding Stationery

A Show Me How DVD Book series

This book and its accompanying DVD are published by

Show Me How Ltd

Champion House, Douglas

Isle of Man, British Isles

IM99 1DD

www.showmehow.im

978-1-84764-001-7

Text, design, filming and photography

copyright@2008 Show Me How Ltd

Disclaimer: Information given in this book is to the author's best knowledge and every effort has been made to ensure accuracy and safety but neither the author nor publisher can be held responsible for any resulting injury, damage or loss to either persons or property. Any further information which will assist in updating of any future editions would be gratefully received.

Follow all health and safety guidelines and, where necessary, obtain health and safety information from the suppliers.

Printed in China

CONTENTS

INTRODUCTION

6 Planning
8 Mass production
10 Cards, envelopes and inserts

PROJECTS

Rosebud Invitation
14

Photo Invitation
20

Pressed Daisy Cards
28

'Swing Tag' Invitation
34

Paper Heart Cards
42

'Wedding Day' Invitation
48

Stamped Heart Cards
52

BASIC SKILLS

56 Making your own cards
58 Mass production techniques
60 Printing photos using a computer
62 Paper and card
63 Wording an invitation
64 Index
Acknowledgments

INTRODUCTION

With such a special event to look forward to, it's important to create a memento to treasure

The invitations to the wedding ceremony or reception are the first things that most of your guests will see, and are your first opportunity to set the theme for the event.

As well as telling guests when and where the marriage is taking place, the invitation is also the perfect way to let everyone know whether to expect a formal occasion, an intimate event for family and close friends, or something more casual and informal.

MAKING WEDDING STATIONERY

Of course, you can have wedding invitations and other stationery professionally printed, but it's very satisfying – and much more personal – to make them yourself. Hand crafting your own cards or outer sleeves, or making them for friends or family, means that you can make something very special – perhaps incorporating initials or photographs to make the invitations unique to yourself, or the bridal couple. Even if you have a large number of cards to send out, you can base them on ready-made, ready-folded card blanks, so you can spend your time on the important personal touches rather than on folding a lot of card. Using a computer, you can add printed messages that will look every bit as finished as those from a print shop – or you can hand-write the inserts for the ultimate in personalised invitations.

Show Me How: Wedding Stationery is the ideal way to find out what's involved in making your own stationery, with lots of ideas for different styles of cards that you can adapt so they will be unique to you. And because everything is shown step-by-step on the DVD, you'll have confidence that every card you make will be the perfect reminder of a very special day.

Planning

Start by making a list of guests, making a note of who you would like to come to the ceremony as well as to the reception. This will give you a guide to how many invitations you

need. Individuals need their own card, but you will only need to send one per couple or family if you are inviting them together. Plan to make a few extra invitations for the couple and the bride's family to keep as mementos, too. It is good etiquette to send an invitation card to the groom's parents, even if it is automatically assumed that they are coming. Many people also like to send invitations to special friends and relatives, even if it is very unlikely that they will be able to attend.

Invitations should normally be sent out around eight weeks before the wedding. This will give the guests plenty of time to plan their diaries and accept the invitation. Anyone needing to make long-distance travel

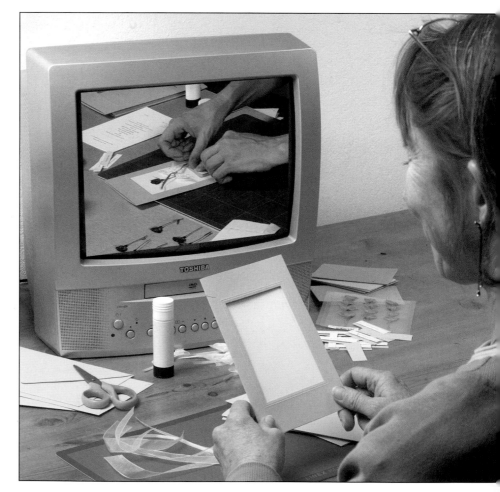

◔*All the skills you need to create beautiful cards and envelopes are clearly demonstrated on the* Show Me How: Wedding Stationery *DVD.*

Attention to detail

Although many weddings are far less formal than they once were, it's still important to send everyone proper details to avoid confusion – and invitation cards are still the best way to do this. Even if you have already spoken to everyone who is coming, or sent out an email confirmation, following this up with a card looks much better and means that all your guests have a reminder of exactly what to expect. Formal etiquette is to mail all the invitations, even though it may seem more logical to hand-deliver those to neighbours and friends.

Things to include on your invitation:

◆ Whether the guest is being invited just to the reception, or to the ceremony as well

◆ What type of event it is – formal or casual

◆ Whether they can bring a partner or not

◆ The date and time of the wedding, and of the reception

◆ Details of the venue

◆ Who is hosting the wedding (and where to send an acceptance)

You'll find text templates for a variety of invitation wordings on page 63.

arrangements may need even more notice. Where fewer guests are going to be invited to the ceremony than the reception, it is a good idea to send out the invitations to the wedding itself well before those for the reception. Then, if some of the guests have to decline, you can invite others who you might otherwise have only been able to invite for the reception.

Making preparations

You need to allow yourself plenty of time to buy the cards, envelopes, paper and other craft materials to make the cards, plus time to prepare the messages and assemble the invitations. This will depend to some degree on how many invitations you are sending, but starting the preparations about four weeks before you need to post them (12 weeks before the wedding itself) should leave plenty of time.

Remember to include copies of maps or relevant directions by road, rail or even plane for those having to travel long distances. It's also a good idea to check availability at a few local hotels or guest houses and include their addresses and contact details, too, to make thing easier for any wedding guests who might require overnight accommodation.

⬆ *Once you have chosen the design you want to make, take a little time to plan which elements can be mass produced. Set aside some time to do this in stages before starting to assemble your cards.*

Mass production

If you are planning a small wedding, you will have plenty of time to handcraft each card individually. But if you have a hundred or so invitations to send out, it pays to set up a system. For example, if the finishing touch is to close the card using a ribbon tied in a bow, it's much easier if you cut all the ribbons to length together, then tie up all the finished cards in one go, instead of going through the whole process of making each card individually. It's an ideal opportunity for family members and friends to pitch in and lend a hand, with one person completing the inserts, another folding the cards and another sealing and addressing envelopes, for example.

Each set of project notes shows how to make a single card, but there is also advice on making multiple cards on pages 58-59.

Other wedding stationery

Most of the projects show how you can make handcrafted invitation cards for the ceremony and supplementary invitations for the reception. We also show some examples of how to make matching 'Thank You' cards that can be sent out after the event, perhaps enclosing a photograph as a reminder of the day.

The same projects can easily be adapted to other wedding stationery, just by changing the printed inserts. Other personalised wedding stationery can include:

◆ Response cards, pre-printed to accept the invitation

◆ Order of service sheets (by arrangement with the minister or registrar)

◆ Menus for the reception

Forward planning

Plan which elements of your chosen design can be prepared in advance to make producing a quantity of invitations much simpler. For example, if you plan to press flowers yourself, you will need to pick them in peak condition in the relevant season (possibly some time in advance), and press a greater quantity than you will need to allow for damage to the blooms. Bows can be made up in quantity in advance and motifs can be punched out of paper and stored flat in a box until needed. For more advice, see the Basic Skills section.

Cards, envelopes and inserts

As it is difficult to print neat messages on thick, decorative card, it's quite usual for wedding invitations to consist of two parts; an outer card or sleeve, plus a printed insert. The projects in this DVD book use ready-made folded blanks, which you can buy from wedding suppliers and stationers. Folded cards come in two forms, either with a single fold down one side, or two flaps that fold in like the double doors of a wardrobe. If you don't want to use ready-made cards, you can make your own, using any decorative card material that you like. There is advice on cutting and folding on page 56, and a guide to paper and envelope sizes on page 62. Inserts can be made from matching or contrasting heavy writing paper (usually white, ivory or cream), either folded or as a single sheet. If you are going to print them, look for paper suitable for an ink-jet or laser printer, depending on which type you are planning to use.

Posting invitations

Matching envelopes are normally available from the same suppliers as the blank cards. Some of them are suitable for sending through the post as they are, although you may find it difficult to write addresses on very decorative papers. In this case, either use sticky address labels, or enclose the envelope in a larger envelope for mailing. Where a card has a very decorative envelope, including features such as ribbon-tied flaps, it will also need to be mailed in a larger, separate envelope. It's a good idea to mock up a complete card with all its component parts and weigh this to

check postage costs. If you are on the brink of paying a higher postage rate, a minor adjustment to the design of the card may help to reduce this.

If the envelopes that match your chosen stationery are elaborate or decorated, post them in a separate, larger envelope to avoid damage in transit. Use pre-printed or hand-written labels on textured or shiny envelopes, where it would be difficult to write legibly directly on to the surface.

Printing inserts

The easiest way to produce neat, clear invitations is to print the inserts using a word processor. Page 63 gives you advice on suitable wording – and if you are buying ready-made blanks, you may also find that templates for popular word-processing programs are provided by the manufacturer. The style of the text will be dictated by the fonts that are available in your word processor. Script typefaces are commonly used for wedding stationery, but you may not have anything suitable, and such fonts can be difficult to read. If in doubt, it is best to avoid quirky typefaces and go for something plain and formal but easily readable, such as Times.

Whether you use a template or not, print out a test page on ordinary paper before printing an insert. This will save wasting an insert if anything goes wrong. Read through carefully to make sure there are no spelling errors or other mistakes such as a wrong date, time or address. Get someone else to check it, too; it's all too easy to overlook a mistake in something you typed yourself. Try the insert against the card to check that the positioning is correct. It may take more than one go to get it right.

In some cases, the best way to print inserts is to do two or three side-by-side on a larger piece of paper and trim this to size. In this case, make doubly sure that the text is positioned correctly.

Adding the names

With a printed insert, you just need to write the guests' names in the space provided. It's best to use a nice pen, rather than a ballpoint, and get someone with neat handwriting to help if your own is untidy. You could print the names if you want, although it means changing the text on every printout, rather than just printing out multiple copies.

There's a neat trick that you can also try if you don't think your handwriting looks good enough. Use a word processor to print the insert in a script face and, instead of printing it in a solid colour, print in a pale grey. Then you can go over the text with a pen, which will hide the faint

A script typeface adds an elegant touch to an invitation. Check that all the letters, including capitals, are easy to read.

guidelines. Once again, you will only want to do this for a small number of special invites.

If you have neat handwriting and you don't have too many invitations to do, you may prefer to hand-write the whole insert. You will need to do a test piece or two to make sure you get the spacing right, and you may need to rule faint pencil lines on the insert to act as guides. Alternatively, enlist the help of someone who can do calligraphy for a really impressive finishing touch.

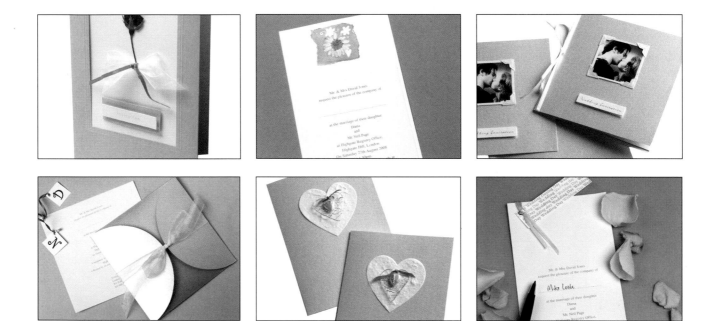

PROJECTS

Rosebud invitation

PERFECTLY PRETTY WITH A CLASSIC RED ROSE

Romantic in pink with touches of organza and satin, and a deep red rosebud

A delightful and simple design, featuring a pressed rosebud decorated with an organza bow with satin ribbon trails and an 'Invitation' label which stands proud of the card in a 3-D effect.

As an unusual extra touch, put a small handful of rose-petal confetti inside each invitation as a surprise for the recipient.

MAKING THE ROSEBUD INVITATION

WHAT YOU NEED

- Pink window card, 18 x 11.5cm
- White insert, 15 x 10cm
- Pressed mini rose
- 18cm of white 1cm-wide organza ribbon
- 15cm of 3mm-wide satin ribbon
- Pink strip of card, 2 x 5.5cm
- Pre-prepared 'Invitation' print
- Printed invitation insert
- Rose-petal confetti
- Paper glue, PVA glue and cocktail stick, glue dot, foam adhesive pads

GETTING STARTED

Apply paper glue around the inside edge of the aperture of a window card and stick the plain white insert in place. Glue the back flap of the card to the back of the window.

ATTACHING THE ROSE

1 Use a cocktail stick to spread PVA glue sparingly on the back of the rosebud. Stick on to the white insert.

Make a single card in around 10 minutes. Pre-prepare all the elements to cut this time down when making a quantity.

MAKING THE BOW

1 Form the length of white organza into two overlapping loops and knot narrow pink ribbon around the middle to form a bow. Clip the ends diagonally.

2 Use a small piece of foam adhesive pad or a glue dot to attach the bow to the lower part of the stem.

EXPERT TIP

◆ You can also buy packets of ready-made bows from haberdashery departments.

FINISHING TOUCHES

1 Use a foam adhesive pad to attach the narrow pink strip of card below the flower. Use another foam adhesive pad to attach the 'Invitation' printed strip to the pink strip of card.

2 Apply paper glue to the back of a printed single sheet invite and stick this inside the card. Fill in the recipient's name then add a handful of rose-petal confetti and put the card inside the envelope.

Photo Invitation

THE PERSONAL TOUCH FOR A UNIQUE INVITATION

Choose a striking and personal monochrome image to create this invitation with a clean, modern feel

This is a very simple and very personal invitation design made using a picture of the bride and groom, but you could use any other suitable black-and-white photograph instead.

The photo is attached to the front of the card using photo corners, and a printed 'Wedding Invitation' label is attached beneath it using a foam adhesive pad to give a raised, 3-D effect. The pre-printed invitation insert is glued in place and held with a decorative narrow satin ribbon. The envelope is finished with a miniature version of the same photographic image.

MAKING THE PHOTO INVITATION

WHAT YOU NEED

◆ Pearlised cream card blank, 12.5 x 12.5cm

◆ Printed photos (see below)

◆ Photo corners

◆ Plain paper

◆ 4mm-wide white ribbon

◆ 'Wedding Invitation' labels

◆ Small foam adhesive pads

◆ Pre-printed invitation insert

◆ Craft knife, metal ruler, cutting mat, scissors

GETTING STARTED

Ideally, use a photo of the bride and groom for this, scanned into the computer and printed out on good quality photographic paper at a suitable size. If you don't have one available you could use any other suitable black-and-white picture instead.

Printing the photos

Start by choosing – or taking – a photo of the bride and groom, or another suitable romantic image. It doesn't matter how big it is, and whether you want to use the whole picture or just part of it. It doesn't even have to be black and white. You can make the picture any size you want, crop out part of a larger image or even print a colour image in black and white.

If you have access to a computer and a little basic knowledge, it is fairly simple to do all this yourself (see Basic Skills pages 60-61 for a step-by-step guide on how to do this). If not, take the photo to a high-street photo shop or copy shop and ask them to do it for you. Explain what you are trying to do and get them to show you samples of the paper they propose using to make sure it is suitable for your cards. You also need to work out how many copies you need for the cards you are making, and how many will fit on a single sheet.

CHOOSING A GREAT PHOTO FOR YOUR INVITE

Suitable images could be traditional ones such as wedding rings or champagne glasses, or a picture of the church or reception venue, or an image of the bridal couple in relaxed mood – on holiday, perhaps.

PREPARING THE CARD

1 Print out the photo on good quality photographic paper, sized to 5cm square. Using a craft knife, metal ruler and a cutting mat, cut out the photo leaving a narrow (2-3mm) white border all around it.

2 To make a template to help you position the photo squarely, cut a 12.5 x 12.5cm square of paper. Cut a 5.5cm square centred 2cm down from the top edge. Lay the template over the front of the card.

ATTACHING THE PHOTO

3 Moisten the photo corners and slide one on to each corner of the photo. Position the photo centrally within the cut-out and press the photo corners down firmly to hold it in place.

4 Apply small foam adhesive pads to the back of a pre-printed 'Wedding Invitation' label and stick this centrally underneath the photo, closer to the lower edge of the card.

ADDING THE INSERT

1 Take a folded insert, cut a little smaller than the actual card, apply paper glue in a line along the back folded edge and stick inside the card.

2 Tie white 4mm-wide ribbon around the fold of the card and knot to form a bow centrally at the front. Cut the ends diagonally.

Pressed Daisy Card

DELIGHTFUL DAISIES FOR A VERY SPECIAL DAY

This design is simple to create and the perfect choice if you need to produce a lot of stylish invitations on a tight budget

Pressed daisies and gold giftwrap are the simple items used to decorate this set of wedding stationery. The single card invitation is printed on pale cream paper and stuck to matching card, and a pressed daisy is set on a torn square of gold giftwrap at the top of the card.

The invitation card slips inside a decorated outer sleeve, tied with gold organza ribbon. The envelope is sealed with a daisy-decorated square of giftwrap to match the invitation card.

The set includes a smaller card suitable for the bride and groom to use as a 'thank you' card.

MAKING THE PRESSED DAISY STATIONERY

WHAT YOU NEED

◆ **Invitation card**
Cream card insert 9.5 x 20.5cm
Gold wedding design gift wrap
Pressed daisy flower heads
Pre-printed invitation

◆ **Outer sleeve**
Cream 21 x 10cm wardrobe-fold
outer sleeve
Gold wedding design gift wrap
1.5cm-wide gold organza ribbon

◆ **Thank-you card**
Cream 10.5 x 7.5cm card blank
Gold wedding design gift wrap
Pressed daisy flower heads
Pre-printed insert

◆ Cutting mat, craft knife, PVA glue,
cocktail stick, paper glue, pencil

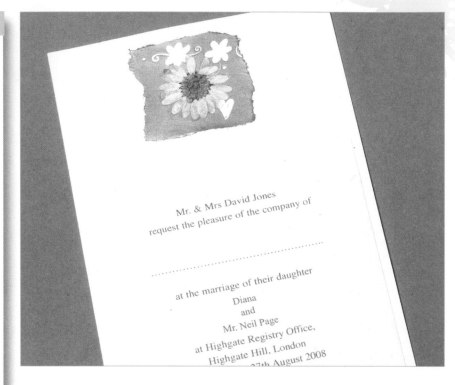

GETTING STARTED

If you are going to make a lot of these invitations,
it's worth thinking ahead and pressing your own
daisies for use. Place the flower heads between
sheets of blotting paper in a flower press or under a
pile of heavy books for 2-3 weeks.

MAKING THE INVITATION CARD

1 Hand tear a strip of gold gift wrap, then tear out a
4cm square so you have torn edges on all sides.
Stick to the top of the card insert with paper glue.

Allow about 15 minutes to make a single invite inner plus decorated outer sleeve; mass production will shorten this.

2 Stick a pressed daisy on the gold torn paper square with PVA glue. Use a cocktail stick to apply the PVA sparingly, taking it to the ends of the petals.

3 Apply paper glue to the back of a printed invite and stick this below the gold paper square and the daisy on the insert. Fill in the name of the recipient.

MAKING THE OUTER SLEEVE

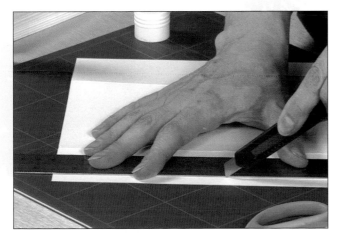

1 To make the decorated outer sleeve, open the blank wardrobe-fold sleeve out flat on a cutting mat. Use a pencil to mark two 2cm slits 1cm in from the opening edges, centred vertically. Use a craft knife and metal ruler to cut the slits.

2 Tear strips of gold gift wrap about 2cm wide between your fingers, so that you have a torn edge on each side. Stick to each front half of the outer sleeve with paper glue. Fold the outer, turn over and cut away the ends of the strips level with the outer with a craft knife.

ADDING THE DAISIES

3 Stick a pressed daisy on to each torn paper strip with PVA glue, using a cocktail stick to spread the glue sparingly and evenly on the back of the flower, starting in centre and taking it to the ends of the petals.

4 Put the prepared insert in place inside the decorated outer sleeve. Thread 25cm of 1.5cm-wide gold organza ribbon through the slits and knot. Cut the ribbon ends on the diagonal.

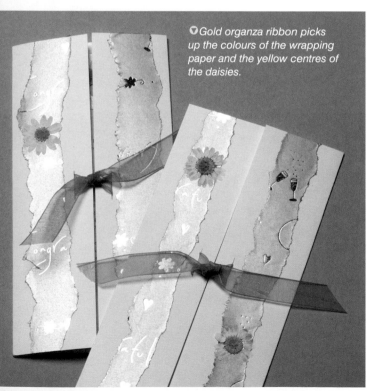

❥ *Gold organza ribbon picks up the colours of the wrapping paper and the yellow centres of the daisies.*

EXPERT TIP

To tear paper, start about 5cm in from the edge of the piece, grasp the top of the paper firmly between thumb and forefinger and tear away from you, using a smooth unhurried action. Move your thumb and forefinger down the strip as you work, and use the other hand to help guide the strip. Turn the paper at the bottom and tear the strip back up, to keep the white edges on the discarded paper.

MAKING THE THANK-YOU CARD

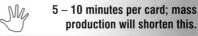

5 – 10 minutes per card; mass production will shorten this.

1 Tear a strip of gold gift wrap about 2cm wide between your fingers. Stick to the left hand edge of the card front with paper glue. Cut the ends level with the card with a craft knife.

2 Stick a pressed daisy on the torn paper strip with PVA glue. Glue a folded, pre-printed insert in place with paper glue, applying a line of glue to the back of the folded sheet.

Using hand-torn strips of gift wrap makes every card unique, as you will always use a different area of the printed design from the paper.

ALTERNATIVES

You can use other types of flower for your design – look out for pressed pansies or the smaller (and appropriately named) heartsease. Combine these with gift wrap in colours appropriate to the flower.

...AND THE ENVELOPES

Tear a 4cm square of gold gift wrap between your fingers. Stick to a sealed envelope with paper glue. Stick a pressed daisy on the torn paper square with PVA glue.

Mr. & Mrs David Jones
request the pleasure of the company of

Tony and Beryl Wright

at the marriage of their daughter
Diana
and
Mr. Neil Page
Highgate Registry Office,
Highgate Hill, London
on Saturday 27th August 2008
at 1.30pm.
A reception will be held afterwards at
Highgate School,
followed by an evening of music and dance

23 Green St
London
W1 2GH
Tel: 020 7631

R.S.V.P.

D N

Swing Tag Invitation

*T*NITIALS ANNOUNCING THE HAPPIEST OF DAYS

Make a feature of the bride's and groom's initials, stamped in a classic script on swing tags, to adorn this stationery set

This personalised invitation features the initials of the bride and groom, stylishly stamped in black on white card and attached to the printed invitation with narrow pink ribbon.

An outer sleeve made of silver card with curved flaps folds around the invitation card and delicate organza ribbon ties in a bow around it.

The bride's and groom's initials feature on the smaller 'thank-you' card too. Ribbon-tied stamped tags are attached to the card, which is tucked into a stamped and be-ribboned outer sleeve.

MAKING THE SWING TAG INVITATION

GETTING STARTED

Look for the unusual curved-flap outer sleeves in wedding stationery suppliers. Alternatively, make your own – see p 57 of the Basic Skills section for a guide on how to do this.

WHAT YOU NEED

◆ **Large inner card**

14 x 14cm white pre-printed invitation card

Additional white card

3mm-wide pink satin ribbon

◆ **Large curved-flap sleeve**

Silver 14.5cm square (closed) outer sleeve

80cm length of white 1.5cm-wide organza ribbon

◆ **Thank-you card**

9 x 9cm white pre-printed thank-you card

Additional white card

3mm-wide pink satin ribbon

◆ **Small outer sleeve**

White 9.5cm square (closed) outer sleeve

3mm-wide pink satin ribbon

◆ Craft knife, cutting mat, single hole punch, scissors, initials rubber stamps, black ink pad

MAKING THE SWING TAGS

EXPERT TIP

◆ Keep wet wipes to hand when stamping, in case you get ink on your fingers and smudge this on to any of the cards.

1 Cut two 2.5cm squares of white card. Stamp the initials of the bride and groom in black on each square. Allow the ink to dry before punching the holes.

A single card will take about 10 minutes. Mass producing the components will make it quicker to make several cards.

2 Resting on a cutting mat, punch a hole on the left hand corner of the pre-printed inner card and on each stamped square with a 3mm single hole punch.

3 Thread pink 3mm-wide ribbon through hole on inner card. Tie a double knot and tie each of the stamped initial cards on to the ends of the ribbon.

TYING UP THE SLEEVE

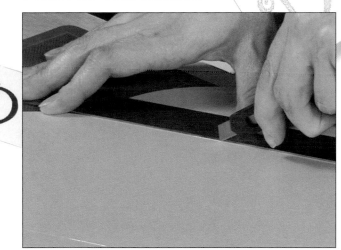

1 Open the curved flaps of the sleeve out flat on a cutting mat. Cut 2cm slits centrally in two opposite creases using a craft knife and metal ruler. Re-fold the sleeve, pressing the creases firmly, then open out again.

EXPERT TIP
◆ Cut the ribbon end to a point to make it easier to thread through holes.

2 Thread 80cm of white 1.5cm-wide organza ribbon through slits. Slip the finished invite under the ribbon. Close the outer flaps, pressing down the folds very firmly, and tie the ribbon in a bow. Trim the ends diagonally.

MAKING THE THANK-YOU CARD

1 Cut two 2.5cm squares of white card. Stamp an initial in black on each square. Use the single hole punch to make a hole in the top left-hand corner of each of the squares.

2 Resting on cutting mat, punch a pair of holes on the left hand edge of the pre-printed thank-you insert about 1.5cm from the top and bottom and a little way in from the side edge, using the single hole punch.

EXPERT TIP

◆ See Basic Skills p 58 for advice on how to make a quantity of these cards by stamping and hole-punching all the tags together.

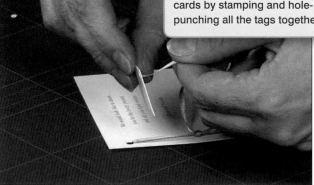

3 Thread a length of pink 3mm-wide ribbon through the holes on the pre-printed insert and tie in a central knot. Knot the stamped initial squares on to each of the free ends of the ribbon.

MAKING THE CARD SLEEVE

A single card will take about 10 minutes. Mass producing the components will make it quicker to make several cards.

1 Pre-fold the outer sleeve, pressing along the creases of the folds very firmly with your finger. Stamp the initials of the bride and groom in black on two opposite flaps. Leave the ink to dry.

> **EXPERT TIP**
>
> ◆ An alphabet set of rubber stamps in an appealing script face is a worthwhile investment: it will come in useful for other projects, too.

2 Resting on a cutting mat, open out the card and punch a hole close to the meeting edge of one of the stamped flaps using a 3mm single hole punch. Fold in the flaps, mark where to position the other punched hole, then open out the flaps and punch it.

3 Put the finished thank-you insert in place, tucking in the stamped tags, then fold up the top and bottom flaps, and then the side ones. Thread pink 3mm-wide ribbon through the holes and tie into a bow. Trim the ends on the diagonal.

Paper Heart Cards

RIBBON-TIED HEARTS FOR AN ELEGANT THEME

Hearts are the dominant motif for this set of wedding stationery — appearing in the form of textured paper and also as pearlised beads enmeshed in wire

This set of invitation cards offers the option of two different card designs, which could be used for guests invited to the wedding and reception, or reception only, plus a themed 'Thank You' card for the bride and groom to use after the event.

The first design is on pearlised card and features a pre-cut paper heart decorated with a beaded wire heart. The second design features a wire heart caught by bands of satin ribbon, while a paper heart and pre-printed label are attached to the 'Thank You' card with a narrow satin ribbon. The matching pearlised envelopes are sealed with textured paper hearts.

MAKING THE PAPER HEART CARDS

WHAT YOU NEED

◆ **Paper heart card**
Fine wire and bead heart
Pre-cut paper heart
Pearlised cream folded card blank 15 x 10.5cm
3mm-wide pink satin ribbon
Pre-printed invitation insert

◆ **Ribbon and heart card**
Pearlised cream folded card blank 15 x 10.5cm
70cm of 4mm-wide white satin ribbon
Fine wire and bead heart
Pre-printed invitation insert

◆ **Thank-you card**
Pearlised cream folded card blank 10.5 x 7.5cm
Pre-cut 'Thank you' labels
Pre-cut paper heart
3mm-wide pink satin ribbon
Pre-printed insert

◆ **Matching envelopes**
Pre-cut paper hearts

◆ Craft knife, scissors, single hole punch, paper glue

GETTING STARTED

Look out for pre-cut paper hearts in wedding stationers and craft supply shops, along with beaded wire hearts and pre-cut 'Thank you' labels. Alternatively, you could use a computer to create and print your own labels.

THE MAIN DESIGN

1 Resting on a cutting mat, centre the wire heart on top of the pre-cut paper heart. Punch a hole each side of centre inside the curves of the wire heart with a 2mm single hole punch.

The card will take about 10 minutes. To make in quantity, prepare all the cards with inserts and pre-prepare the wire and paper hearts.

2 Thread one end of the length of narrow pink ribbon through the wire heart and the holes in the paper heart and tie with a double knot.

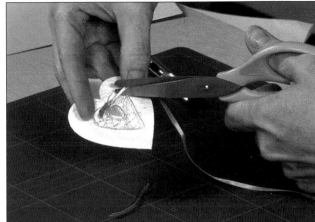

3 Trim the ends of the ribbon diagonally. Apply paper glue to the back of the paper heart and stick it to the front of the pearlised card.

ADDING THE INSERT

4 Trim a pre-printed invitation insert so that it is a little smaller all round than the actual card, and fold in half. Run a line of paper glue along the back of the fold, and stick the insert inside the card.

ALTERNATIVES

◆ If you can't find similar wire hearts you could create them in metal foil, available from craft shops in several colours and suitable for embossing. Or sew decorative beads to hearts cut from pink or red felt.

A single card will take about 10 minutes. Mass producing the components will make it quicker to make several cards.

RIBBON AND HEART CARD

1 Open card out flat on cutting mat. Cut three 4mm slits on fold about 1.5cm below upper edge and 6mm apart. Repeat 6mm in from right hand edge – the slits don't have to line up. Wiggle the craft knife tip a little to enlarge the slits slightly to thread the ribbon through.

2 Thread the ribbon through the top slit at the fold. Thread the other free end through at the opposite side and lace across, catching in a wire heart and joining the free ends in a double knot, close to the point where you started threading the ribbon.

3 Trim the ends of the ribbon diagonally. Add an appropriate folded invitation insert inside the card using paper glue as before.

EXPERT TIP

◆ Cut one end of the ribbon diagonally to help you thread it through the slits – you can re-cut each time if it starts to fray. You can also use the tip of a craft knife to help you thread the ribbon through.

One card will take about 5 minutes. Mass producing the components will make it quicker to make several cards.

THE THANK-YOU CARD

1 Open the smaller pearlised card out flat. Resting on the cutting mat, hold the paper heart and pre-printed 'thank you' label on the front of the card in the top left-hand corner. Punch a hole through both the heart and the label using a 2mm single hole punch.

2 Thread pink 3mm-wide ribbon through the heart and label at the front of the card, bringing it up over the top of the card. Knot the ends and cut them at an angle. Cut a single printed insert sheet to fit. Apply paper glue around the edge on the wrong side and stick in place.

ENVELOPES

◆ To decorate the envelope, stick a strip of double-sided tape on the back of a pre-cut paper heart. Insert the card into the envelope so that the decorated side faces the recipient when they open the envelope. The card back then lies to the front of the envelope, giving a flat surface for the address. Stick the paper heart to the sealed envelope flap.

Mr. & Mrs David Jones
Request the pleasure of the company

..... Mike leslie ....

At the marriage of their daughter
Kate Emelia
With
Mr. Geoffrey Page
at Highgate Registry office,
Highgate Hill, London
On Saturday 27th August 20xx
At 1.30pm.
A reception will be held afterwards at
Highgate School,
followed by an evening of music and dance
Dress Code: Black Tie

'Wedding Day' Invitation

Ribbons and hearts for wedding day style

Cool, modern styling brings a touch of class to this ribbon-tied invitation, set in an embossed outer sleeve decorated with a heart

This invitation is a simple pre-printed sheet decorated with a strip of 'Wedding Day' print, the decorative theme that runs through this project. It is secured inside an embossed wardrobe-folded outer sleeve, tied with a narrow satin ribbon and decorated with a transparent heart backed with the same 'Wedding Day' print.

A matching embossed envelope is decorated with a sticker made of the 'Wedding Day' print bordered with pink to match the ribbons used throughout.

43

MAKING THE INITIALS OUTER SLEEVE

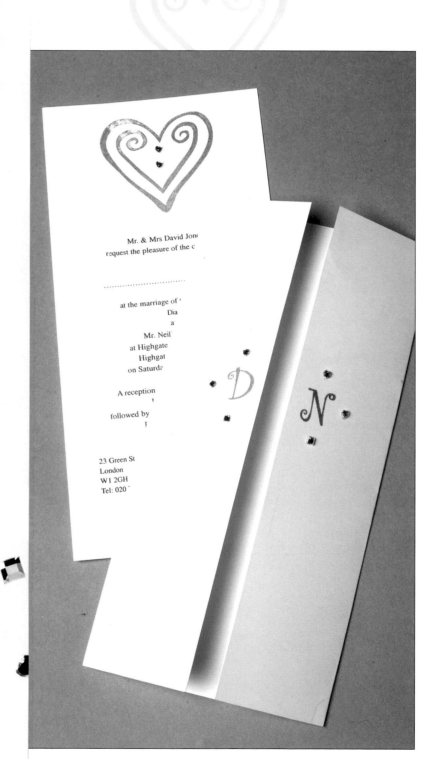

1 Take a pre-folded outer sleeve and stamp the initials of the bride and groom each side of the central opening, using silver metallic ink. Align them by eye just above the half-way point, close to the opening edges.

2 Stick diamanté stickers around the initials, dividing them with a craft knife and using the tip of the knife to lift and place them. Apply them centrally above, below and at the sides of the initials, turning the card as you work. Add the stamped invitation insert to the sleeve.

MAKING THE HEARTS OUTER SLEEVE

1 Place the closed blank outer sleeve on some scrap paper. Stamp randomly over the sleeve front, coating the stamp with ink each time. Vary the angle of the stamps and allow some to overlap the edges of the card on to the scrap paper, and some to 'straddle' the central opening.

ALTERNATIVES

Hearts are a popular motif for weddings, and if you can't find this particular rubber stamp design, you will certainly find plenty of others to choose from.

If you would like a change from hearts, you could stamp the all-over design using the couple's initials or look out for suitable motifs such as champagne glasses, flowers or a wedding cake. If you want something a little different, look for something with a modern twist such as a girly dress or high heel shoes.

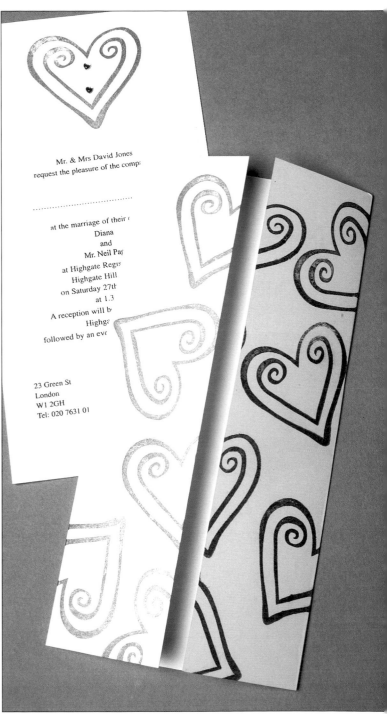

Mr. & Mrs David Jones request the pleasure of the comp:

at the marriage of their
Diana
and
Mr. Neil Pa
at Highgate Regis
Highgate Hill
on Saturday 27t
at 1.3
A reception will b
Highg
followed by an ev

23 Green St
London
W1 2GH
Tel: 020 7631 01

Printing photos using a computer

It's easy to print multiple miniature photos at home using a computer, and much cheaper than getting them done at a photo shop or copy shop. You don't even need a special program – an ordinary word processor will do. It doesn't matter if the photo is in colour. You can make it black and white just by telling the computer to print it that way.

1 Once your picture is on the computer, start your word processor and open a new document.

2 Then put your picture on the page. In Microsoft Word, the command is Insert Picture. Choose From File. Find the picture from where you saved it and click Insert.

3 It will appear actual size on the page, which will probably be much too big, so click on the image to make the frame appear. Then move the mouse to one of the corners. It will change to a pair of scaling arrows. Holding down the mouse button, move these inwards to make the image the size you want, then let go.

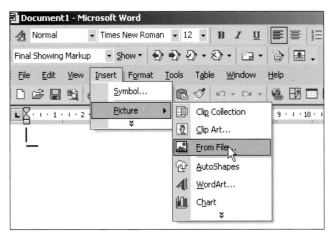

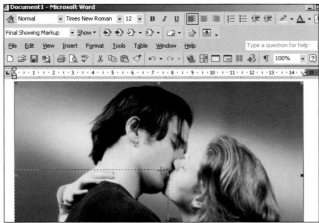

EXPERT TIP

◆ You can reduce your photograph by eye, but if you want to check the size, double-click on the picture. This brings up the Picture toolbar and the Format Picture window.

4 Select the Size tab to see the dimensions. You can change the width or height by typing a dimension in here. So long as Lock Aspect Ratio is ticked, the picture will scale itself in proportion.

CHANGING A COLOUR

◆ To change a colour image to black and white, double-click on the picture to bring up the Picture toolbar and the Format Picture window.

5 Select the Picture tab to see the Color setting under Image Control. Change this from Automatic to Grayscale (not black and white, which will lose all the shading).

6 When you are happy with the picture, select it and do a Copy. Then just Paste it as many times as you want to see rows of images filling the page.

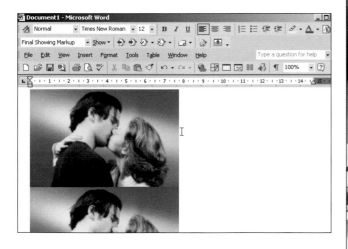

7 Now just print the page. If the original picture had no border, there won't be a gap between the images, so they will be easy to separate with a single cut between them.

Choosing paper and card

When you are buying paper, card and envelopes, or working out how to print on them, it helps to have a basic understanding of how the sizes work.

Paper is most commonly sold in 'A series' sizes. Ordinary computer and writing paper is A4, but there are sizes going from A0 (a poster size) to A10 (about the size of a postage stamp). Each is half the size of the one before, so if you fold the long edge of A4 in half, you get A5. Fold that in half and you get A6.

A4 is 29.7cm x 21cm (297mm x 210mm)

A5 is 21cm x 14.85cm (this may be quoted as 14.5 or 15cm)

A6 is 14.85cm x 10.5cm (again it may be rounded up or down)

There is a matching series of envelopes, sold in C sizes. The formula is simple; an A4 page fits into a C4 envelope, an A5 folded card fits into a C5 and so on. Ordinary letter envelopes are called DL and are designed to take A4 folded in three.

As all these sizes are an international standard, you can mix and match from different sources. There are some less common sizes for both paper and envelopes. Some of these are based on custom sizes and shapes (eg square) so you need to buy both from the same source or check the sizes carefully to be sure of a good fit.

Paper weight and printing

Paper and card thickness is measured in terms of what a square metre weighs. This is quoted in grams per square metre, normally written as gsm or g/m2. Ordinary printer or photocopier paper is 80gsm, 100gsm is a little thicker and stiffer (like a letter-writing paper), 160gsm is a thin card.

Some computer printers cannot handle anything thicker than 160gsm, so if you plan to print parts of your wedding stationery, check this before you

buy the paper. Run a test on a couple of sheets before you [...] the materials in bulk. If the paper wasn't intended for a com[...] printer, you might find that the ink smudges.

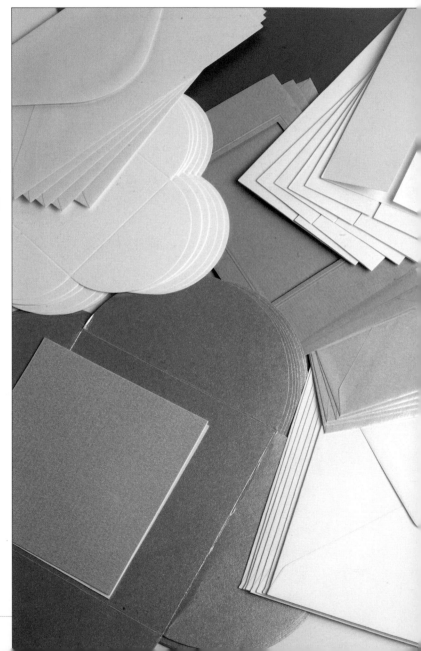

Wording an invitation

These suggestions show how you can word wedding invitations to suit various situations. They follow formal etiquette, but you can amend the wording of these examples to suit your own preferences.

Traditional wedding and reception – formal invitation from the bride's parents*

Mr and Mrs Michael Harrison
request the honour of the presence of

....

at the marriage of their daughter
Diana Catherine
and
Mr Neil Baker
at St Luke's Church
Hadley Road, Worcester WR2 4CA
on Saturday 28th June 2008
at 1:00pm
followed by a reception at
The Bay Tree Hotel
Worcester Road
Evesham WR11 5BD

Please reply to
Mr and Mrs Harrison
15 Milton Gardens
Evesham WR11 9AH

Informal invitation from bride and groom to wedding and reception

Diana Harrison and Mr Neil Baker
would like to invite

....

to their wedding
at Worcester Register Office
119 High Street
Worcester WR1 8PS
on Saturday 28th June 2008
at 11:30am
followed by a reception at
Fellowes Tennis Club
Dorney Road
Worcester WR4 6CS

RSVP
47 Ivy Terrace
Worcester
WR3 6GF

Reception only – formal invitation from the bride's parents

Mr and Mrs Michael Harrison
request the pleasure of the company of

....

at a reception to celebrate the marriage of
their daughter
Diana Catherine
to
Mr Neil Baker
to be held at
The Bay Tree Hotel
Worcester Road
Evesham WR11 5BD
on Saturday 28th June 2008
at 3:30pm

Please reply to
Mr and Mrs Harrison
15 Milton Gardens
Evesham WR11 9AH

---

* Where the wedding is a civil ceremony, it is conventional to use 'request the pleasure of the presence of' in place of 'request the honour of the presence of"

VARIATIONS

These examples show how to adapt a standard invitation to suit differing personal circumstances. They are based on the reception-only invitation.

Invitation from divorced parents

Mr Michael Harrison and Mrs Anne Harrison
request the pleasure of the company of

....

at a reception to celebrate the marriage of
their daughter
(etc)…

Invitation from re-married mother

Mr and Mrs John Hemmings
request the pleasure of the company of

....

at a reception to celebrate the marriage of
her daughter
(etc)…

Invitation from widowed parent

Mrs Michael Harrison
requests the pleasure of the company of

....

at a reception to celebrate the marriage of
her daughter
(etc)…

INDEX

A

Adding insert	23
Add-ons	59

B

Bows preparing	59

C

Cards	
choosing	62
envelopes and inserts	10
make your own	56
mass production	58
Computer printing photos	60
Curved flap card	57
Cutting out motifs	59

D E F

Daisy, see Pressed daisy	
Envelope	29
decorating	47
Forward planning	9

I

Inserts adding	23
adding name	11
printing	11
Invitations	
attention to details	7
choosing paper and card	62
mass production	8, 58
paper heart cards	38
planning	6, 9
posting	10
preparations	7
preparing the card	22
pressed daisy	26
printing inserts	11
ribbon and heart	40
rosebud invitation	16
stamped heart	50
swing tag	32
'Wedding Day'	44
wording	63

M

Make your own cards	56
Making a bow	8, 58

O

Other stationery	44
Outer sleeve	46, 53

P

Paper heart cards	38
insert	38
Photo invitation	
attaching the photo	22
choosing photo	21
printing	60
Planning	6, 9
Posting invitations	10
Preparing the card	22
Pressed daisy invitation	26
Printing	
inserts	11
photos	60

R

Ribbon and heart card	40
envelope	41
Rosebud invitations	16
finishing touch	17
making a bow	17

S

Stamped heart invitation	50
outer sleeve	53
Swing tag invitation	32
card sleeve	35

T

Thank-you card	29, 34, 41
alternative	29
decorating	45
envelopes	29, 41

W

Wardrobe-fold outer sleeve	57
'Wedding Day' invitation	45
Wording an invitation	63

PROJECT SKILL LEVEL

Easy

Moderate

Difficult

ACKNOWLEDGMENTS

Thanks to Cheryl Owen
Picture Credits: p 7: Creasource/CORBIS
Photography: Mike Leale

If you enjoyed this book and DVD, look out for other titles in the Show Me How series

Wedding Stationery
Give your wedding arrangements a personal touch by creating your own handcrafted invitation cards and other wedding stationery.

Wedding Decorations
The perfect guide for anyone who wants to give a wedding reception an individual style by creating their own table settings.

Flower Arranging
Demonstrated by award-winning experts, who show even a complete novice how to create eye-catching designs to suit different sorts of flowers and settings.

Glass Painting
A detailed introduction to this absorbing and creative hobby thats shows how to create eye-catching, beautiful gifts and items for the home.

The Show Me How range includes Crafts and Hobbies, Christmas, Art, Technology, Cooking, Health and many more.
Available from all major book shops and craft shops everywhere.

www.showmehow.im   Show Me How Ltd, Champion House, Douglas, Isle of Man, British Isles, IM99 1DD Tel: 00(44) 01624 640066